Once Upon a Touch...

Ladybird's Remarkable Relaxation
How children (and frogs, dogs, flamingos and dragons) can use yoga relaxation to help deal with stress, grief, bullying and lack of confidence
Michael Chissick
Illustrated by Sarah Peacock
ISBN 978 1 84819 146 4
eISBN 978 0 85701 112 1

Frog's Breathtaking Speech
How children (and frogs) can use yoga breathing to deal with anxiety, anger and tension
Michael Chissick
Illustrated by Sarah Peacock
ISBN 978 1 84819 091 7
eISBN 978 0 85701 074 2

The Mouse's House
Children's Reflexology for Bedtime or Anytime
Susan Quayle
Illustrated by Melissa Muldoon
ISBN 978 1 84819 247 8
eISBN 978 0 85701 193 0

Baby Shiatsu
Gentle Touch to Help your Baby Thrive
Karin Kalbantner-Wernicke and Tina Haase
Illustrated by Monika Werneke
Foreword by Steffen Fischer
ISBN 978 1 84819 104 4
eISBN 978 0 85701 086 5

Indian Head Massage for Special Needs
Giuliana Fenwick
ISBN 9781848192751
eISBN 9780857012227

Qigong Massage for Your Child with Autism
A Home Program from Chinese Medicine
Louisa Silva
Foreword by Anita Cignolini
ISBN 978 1 84819 070 2

Once Upon a Touch...

Story Massage for Children

Mary Atkinson and Sandra Hooper

SINGING
DRAGON
LONDON AND PHILADELPHIA

This edition published in 2016
by Singing Dragon
an imprint of Jessica Kingsley Publishers
73 Collier Street
London N1 9BE, UK
and
400 Market Street, Suite 400
Philadelphia, PA 19106, USA

www.singingdragon.com

First published in 2014 by RedDoor

Library of Congress Cataloging in Publication Data
A CIP catalog record for this book is available from the Library of Congress

British Library Cataloguing in Publication Data
A CIP catalogue record for this book is available from the British Library

ISBN 978 1 84819 287 4
eISBN 978 0 85701 234 0

Printed and bound in China

This book is dedicated to:

Alex
Charlie
Emma
Lizi

Acknowledgements

We've been supported and inspired by many people, both adults and children, who have generously shared their time, expertise and experience to help create *Once Upon a Touch... Story Massage for Children*. It is wonderful to know that so many others feel as enthusiastic about story massage as we do.

We would like to give special thanks to Alice Clarke for creating such beautiful illustrations for the book and to Graham at Nicky Linzey Design for designing the symbols for our strokes.

Some of the massage stories included in this book are written by friends and colleagues including: Gaynor and Jeran Entwistle, Kim Hart and the children at Wallands Community School, Lyn Holmes, Katy Lassetter, Nerine Standen, Joanne Turner, Sarah Williams, Angela Vigus and Beverly Pearson.

Others have contributed ideas and valuable feedback including: Takiko Ando, Emma Atkinson, Helen Booth, Meg Fenn, Lola Fernandez, Nicky Hales, Mandy Humphrey, Toni McGloin, Adam Parker, Angela Philpott, Alice Readman, Sally Reynolds, Keiko Sugawara, Ali Marson, Catriona Plunkett and everyone at Golden Egg Holistic.

Contents

Introduction   9

How to Use This Book   11

Benefits of Story Massage for Children   13

Suggested Guidelines   15

The Ten Massage Strokes   18

The Massage Stories   29

Story Massage in Action   30

Traditional Tales   32
Twinkle, Twinkle, Little Star   33
Humpty Dumpty   34
Hickory Dickory Dock   35
Cinderella   36
Little Red Riding Hood   38
St George and the Dragon   40

Seasonal Strokes   42
Tick Tock, Watch the Clock   43
Pancake Song   44
In the Springtime   46
Grandad Grows Potatoes   47
Remember, Remember the Fifth of November   48
Countdown to Christmas   49

In Your Imagination 50

Can You Hear the Music? 51

Ahoy There! 52

Fun at the Fair 54

Kelly's Balloon Ride 56

Flash the Aeroplane 58

The Circus Comes to Town 59

Adding a Personal Touch 60

Let's Bake a Birthday Cake 61

Freddie's Bathtime 62

Ben Goes on the Bus 64

Olly Goes Fishing 65

Alice Plays Football 66

Team Effort 68

Hands-on Learning 70

Walking on the Moon 71

Great Fire of London 72

Deep in the Rainforest 73

Greek Myths 76

Winding Rivers 78

Growing Sunflowers 79

Time for Talking 80

Animal Friends 81

A Safe Place 82

The Inquisitive Iguanodon 84

The Frightened Ghost 86

First Day at Forest School 87

About the Authors 88

Introduction

We all love stories. When combined with the benefits of simple massage strokes, stories present wonderful opportunities for creativity and interaction.

Story massage involves the use of easy-to-follow massage strokes associated with spoken words that help to build up an engaging story. The strokes in this book are shown on shoulders, back, arms and head. They can easily be adapted for hands, feet, legs and face as appropriate. No oil is used and children do not remove any clothes.

Movements and stories can be adapted to suit the individual needs of children of varying ages, abilities, personalities and temperaments.

When sharing story massage you can choose positions that are the most comfortable and suitable for the situation. You can sit, lie down or stand, work one-on-one or in a line or circle. Story massage is an activity to be enjoyed whenever or wherever the time feels right. The emphasis is on sharing the many benefits of nurturing and positive touch.

How to Use This Book

Once Upon a Touch… Story Massage for Children begins with a basic explanation of why positive touch has such far-reaching benefits for children. Story massage can be enjoyed with the minimum of preparation. However, to ensure maximum benefits we have included some basic guidelines for safe and respectful touch.

We then offer step-by-step instructions for ten imaginative strokes that form the basis of the massage stories in this book. These strokes can be used to represent a choice of objects, actions and emotions in a story massage. Each stroke is accompanied by a symbol and variations of the stroke. Here, for example, is the symbol for the stroke called The Circle, with variations.

Central to the book is a collection of original story massages written with the help and advice of both children and adults. These stories will help build confidence with story massage and provide a valuable resource for on-going participation, whether at home or in the classroom. The stories vary in length and complexity; some contain only a few strokes and take less than 30 seconds to complete.

Others may take up to a couple of minutes and involve most, or all, of the strokes.

The story massages in *Once Upon a Touch… Story Massage for Children* comprise written words to be read aloud accompanied by a series of massage strokes. Each line of the story is enhanced by a corresponding massage stroke. To make it simple to follow, the symbol for the stroke is placed on the left hand side of the appropriate line. Once you become familiar with these story massages, you may choose to begin personalising the words or creating new stories based on favourite books, activities or projects. Stories can be linked to the school curriculum or tailored to meet the specific needs of a child. Children can be encouraged to participate in storytelling and draw their own illustrations for massage stories.

Benefits of Story Massage for Children

Story massage offers a simple, fun and interactive way of sharing the benefits of positive touch with children of all ages and abilities. The benefits will obviously vary depending on the situation, whether at home, in the classroom or other location, and also the responses and particular needs of the individual child, but may include:

- The relaxation of mind and body, easing tension and the cumulative effects of stress.

- The promotion of 'feel-good' hormones including oxytocin, which help to boost general well-being.

- The opportunity for children to experience dedicated 'calming time'.

- Learning the essential life skill of conscious relaxation through first-hand experience of the benefits of recharging and refreshing mind and body.

- Improved alertness and concentration.

- Reduction of aggressive and hyperactive behaviour.

- An increased sensitivity by children of how their own actions and emotions can influence those of others.

- Increased self-confidence, self-awareness and self-esteem.

- An alternative and engaging way of encouraging children to develop a wider vocabulary.

- The opportunity for children to practically engage in experiences that provide a context for the use of emotional language.

- Individual attention that enhances a child's awareness of being valued, and brings a sense of self-worth.

- A fun way for families and friends to share time together and connect with each other.

- The opportunity to encourage children to develop their imagination.

Suggested Guidelines

Suggestions for how to use story massage depend on whether you are introducing peer massage to a group of children in a school or community setting, sharing story massage with a child at home or working in a completely different environment such as a hospital or hospice. Age, ability and personality must also be taken into consideration. However, following these important guidelines will enhance the positive effects of story massage for everyone.

Showing Respect

- Story massage should never be forced on a child. Before each session begins, children should be asked whether they would like to have a story massage, and respect should be shown for their right to decline. Depending on the situation, children who do not wish to participate may be invited to sit quietly and listen to the words of the story or watch others taking part. Alternatively, they may wish to do the massage strokes in the air or experience the strokes by doing them on themselves.

- At the end of the session, the person giving the story massage should thank the person receiving the massage. The appreciation is usually reciprocated.

- During the session, the child receiving a story massage should be invited to share what feels good about the massage or what could be changed. The person giving the story massage respects these comments. It is important to listen to verbal feedback or body language and consider adjusting the pressure to make it firmer or lighter, changing the movement, altering the position or even stopping the session.

Having Fun

- Story massage is an activity to be enjoyed. It is good to laugh together so long as this does not distract others.

- Children should be allowed to learn the moves at their own pace and in their own way. The intention of story massage is not about achieving perfection but sharing healthy and positive interaction with others.

- Story massage can be enjoyed at any time, but for some children in certain situations it may be beneficial to have a regular time slot. Children usually participate better when they are not feeling over-tired or hungry.

- Story massage is creative and interactive. It is great fun to adapt or invent stories to make them relevant and personal. The stories offered in this book are chosen as suggestions allowing you to develop your own themes and ideas.

Being Cautious

- Always take into account the individual needs and preferences of each child, or group of children. Work within your own framework of expertise, experience and qualifications.

- When using story massage as a positive touch activity outside the family home, it is vital to be aware of any policies or protocols in place within the particular setting in which you are working.

The Ten Massage Strokes

These ten massage strokes form the basis of the massage stories in *Once Upon a Touch… Story Massage for Children*. You will notice that there are also some variations on these basic strokes, which are designed to help expand the scope for creativity within story massage. You may like to practise the strokes and variations first before you begin combining them with the stories.

The basic massage strokes can be used to represent a wide choice of objects, actions and emotions. As you become more familiar with the concept of story massage, you may enjoy using these strokes to devise your own stories or create some new strokes.

The Circle

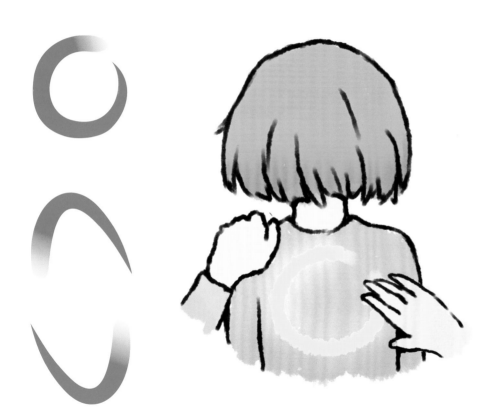

Rest one hand on your partner's shoulder. With the flat of the other hand, make a large, circular movement on the back.

This can be in a clockwise or anti-clockwise direction.

Getting Creative

- Make the circular shape in different sizes.

- Draw a half-circle on the back. This can be facing in different directions.

- Vary the speed and pressure of this move, according to the storyline.

The Wave

Rest one hand on your partner's shoulder. With the flat of the other hand, make a wave-like, zig-zag movement on your partner's back in a downward direction.

Getting Creative

- Make this move in a horizontal direction across the back.

- Use both hands together.

- Vary the speed and pressure of this move, according to the storyline.

The Fan

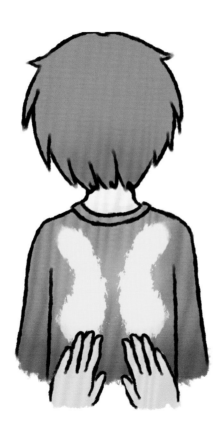

Start with the flats of both hands resting on either side of the spine at the base of your partner's back and pointing upwards. With both hands working at the same time, stroke your hands up your partner's back gently 'fanning' out, finishing at the shoulders.

Getting Creative

- Reverse the move beginning at the top of your partner's back, with your hands either side of the spine. Stroke your hands in a downward direction, 'fanning' outwards.

- Vary the speed and pressure of this move, according to the storyline.

The Walk

Begin by placing the flat of one hand on your partner's back. Now place your other hand nearby in a different place on the back and, at the same time, gently lift the first hand off. Repeat this 'walking' pattern all over the back and arms.

Getting Creative

- Vary the speed and pressure of this move, according to the storyline.

The Drum

With both hands held in loosely clenched fists and with hands moving one after the other, gently 'drum' all over your partner's back. Avoid the spine.

Getting Creative

- Try this move on your partner's shoulders and arms.

- Try this move with both hands working together.

- Vary the speed and pressure of this move, according to the storyline.

The Claw

Place your hands in the shape of claws with fingers slightly bent and rigid. With both hands on your partner's back, stroke in a downward movement from shoulders to waistline. Maintain the 'claw-like' shape with pads of fingers and thumbs staying in constant contact with the back. Repeat several times.

Getting Creative

- Try this move on your partner's head.

- Make shorter 'clawing' strokes, moving in an upward or downward direction, one hand after the other.

- Vary the speed and pressure of this move, according to the storyline.

The Squeeze

Place both hands on top of your partner's shoulders. Now gently squeeze and release. Repeat this gentle 'squeezing' movement several times.

Getting Creative

- This 'squeezing' movement also feels good on the arms. Begin at the upper arms, one hand on each arm, and move up and down, applying gentle pressure as you go.

The Bounce

With both hands working at the same time, place the pads of the fingers and thumbs on your partner's back. Now gently draw the fingers and thumb of each hand together and lift off quickly. Repeat this 'bouncing' move all over the back.

Getting Creative

- Try this 'bouncing' move on your partner's head, shoulders and arms.

- Vary the speed and pressure of this move, according to the storyline.

The Sprinkle

With both hands working at the same time, lightly tap the pads of your fingers, one finger at a time, in a random fashion all over the back, as if playing the piano. This is a light and gentle movement.

Getting Creative

- Try this 'sprinkling' movement on your partner's head, shoulders and arms.

The Calm

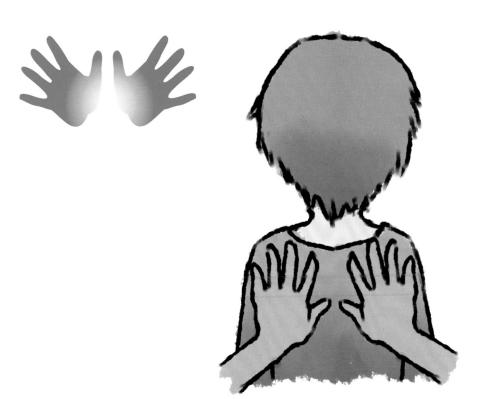

Rest the flats of both hands gently on your partner's back, head or shoulders. Hold for as long as is appropriate for the storyline.

Getting Creative

- Use the flat of one hand only.
- Try this on the upper arms or over the ears.

The Massage Stories

One of the joys of story massage is that there is such a wealth of inspiration for themes and subjects.

Everything, from the everyday to the extraordinary and the familiar to the fantastic, can be used as a storyline. Simple massage strokes are chosen to complement the spoken words and bring the story to life. Story massage can be celebratory, imaginative, instructive, therapeutic and personal.

Different stories are appropriate for different children and individual settings and occasions. We invite you to adapt, alter or personalise the words or themes of the stories. Similarly, children will enjoy some massage strokes more than others. Take some time to discover which strokes feel more pleasurable to give and receive, and fit in best with the storyline.

The massage stories in *Once Upon a Touch… Story Massage for Children* have been carefully selected to offer an example of some of the many possibilities for story massage. We hope you will find that some of these stories will spark your enthusiasm to begin exploring the wonders of story massage.

Story Massage in Action

The massage stories have been divided into six sections to illustrate the variety of situations to which you can bring story massage:

1. Traditional Tales

This section shows how favourite stories, rhymes and songs can be transformed into simple or more complex story massages.

2. Seasonal Strokes

Celebrating the changing seasons with story massage can add an extra dimension to the anticipation and the experience of the event. It can also provide opportunities for respectful reflection on the ways in which people from different cultures mark special occasions.

3. In Your Imagination

Imagination is integral to stories as we know and love them. These enchanting story massages can stimulate a child's imagination and encourage them to enter a whole new world.

4. Adding a Personal Touch

All children need to feel special. Story massage, made individual to a particular child or group of children, can enhance a child's awareness of being valued and bring a sense of self-worth. These stories are designed for the words to be changed so that you can add a personal touch.

5. Hands-on Learning

A kinaesthetic learning tool, story massage gives children a chance to experience a quiet time in which they can explore curriculum topics in a different way. Children can also be encouraged to create their own story massages around a chosen subject.

6. Time for Talking

Story massage can help build trust through a shared connection. Over time, it can encourage the discussion of concerns and anxieties in a calm, safe atmosphere.

Traditional Tales

- Twinkle, Twinkle, Little Star
- Humpty Dumpty
- Hickory Dickory Dock
- Cinderella
- Little Red Riding Hood
- St George and the Dragon

Twinkle, Twinkle, Little Star

 Twinkle, twinkle, little star,

 how I wonder what you are.

 Up above the world so high,

 like a diamond in the sky.

 Twinkle, twinkle, little star,

 how I wonder what you are.

Humpty Dumpty

 Humpty Dumpty sat on a wall.

 Humpty Dumpty had a great fall.

 All the King's horses,

 and all the King's men,

 couldn't put Humpty together again.

Hickory Dickory Dock

 Hickory Dickory Dock.

 The mouse ran up the clock.

 The clock struck one.

 The mouse ran down.

 Hickory Dickory Dock.

Cinderella

 Once upon a time there lived a beautiful girl who was a servant to her stepmother and stepsisters.

 She was called Cinderella after the cinders that she swept from the fire grate.

 She washed their clothes and did all of the chores without any thanks.

 One day the postman knocked on the door of the house with an invitation to a Grand Ball at the palace.

 Cinderella was sad because she knew that she would not be able to go.

 Then her fairy godmother appeared and waved a magic wand.

Cinderella's dirty old clothes were changed into a beautiful ball gown

 with twinkling glass slippers for her feet.

 At the ball, Cinderella danced and danced with handsome Prince Charming.

 She was very, very happy.

 However, when the clock stuck midnight, Cinderella knew that she must run away or the spell would be broken. She ran so fast that she left a glass slipper behind.

 Prince Charming walked all over the land to find the beautiful maiden whose foot would fit the slipper.

 Finally, he found Cinderella.

 They lived happily ever after.

Little Red Riding Hood

 Little Red Riding Hood walked through the forest to visit her sick granny.

 She took some chocolate cake in a wicker basket.

 On the way a wicked wolf stopped Little Red Riding Hood and asked where she was going.

 'I am taking the winding path that leads to Granny's little cottage,' she said.

 The wicked wolf ran to the cottage and ate Granny up.

 Then the wolf put on Granny's cap,

 and her shawl,

 and lay down under the blankets on Granny's bed and waited for the little girl to arrive.

Little Red Riding Hood tiptoed quietly into Granny's bedroom.

 'Granny, what big ears you have!' she said. 'All the better to hear you with,' replied the wicked wolf.

 'Granny, what big eyes you have!' said Little Red Riding Hood. 'All the better to see you with,' replied the wolf.

 'Granny, what big teeth you have!' said Little Red Riding Hood. 'Grrr! All the better to eat you with!' said the wolf.

 Then the wolf swallowed Little Red Riding Hood down in one gulp,

 and fell asleep on the bed.

 Some time later, a woodsman came by and cut the wolf open with his axe.

 Out jumped Granny and Little Red Riding Hood!

 Then they all sat down and enjoyed the chocolate cake for tea.

St George and the Dragon

 There once lived a fierce dragon with scary claws and teeth.

 One day, a princess cried 'Please don't eat me!'

 The dragon terrorised everyone in the land.

 'I will save you,' said St George arriving on his horse.

 When he was angry, the dragon spat flames of fire from his great big mouth.

 St George bravely struck the dragon with his spear.

 When he was hungry, the dragon swallowed young maidens into his great big belly.

 The dragon roared and spluttered poison over St George.

They fought and fought,

 The young princess was saved.

 all through the day, and all through the night

 Everyone danced and cheered.

 until silence fell upon the land.

 The terrible dragon was dead.

 St George had slayed the dragon!

 They all gave thanks to brave St George.

Seasonal Strokes

- Tick Tock, Watch the Clock
- Pancake Song
- In the Springtime
- Grandad Grows Potatoes
- Remember, Remember the Fifth of November
- Countdown to Christmas

Tick Tock, Watch the Clock

 Tim looks up at the clock and thinks about the day.

 Maybe it will be warm enough to swim in the pool...

 Will he play on his trampoline?

 and he can practice his diving.

 Will he go with his friends to fly their kites?

 Maybe he will go climbing.

 Will he go with his sister for a walk in the wood?

 Be careful not to fall!

 Perhaps he will have his favourite food.

 Yippee, it's the school holidays, there's time to do it ALL!

Pancake Song

Pop a little pancake into a pan.
Pop a little pancake into a pan.
Pop a little pancake into a pan.

It's for my dinner today.

Toss a little pancake out of the pan. Toss a little pancake out of the pan. Toss a little pancake out of the pan.

It's for my dinner today.

Squeeze a little lemon, squeeze, squeeze, squeeze. Squeeze a little lemon squeeze, squeeze, squeeze. Squeeze a little lemon, squeeze, squeeze, squeeze.

It's for my dinner today.

Shake a little sugar, shake, shake, shake. Shake a little sugar, shake, shake, shake. Shake a little sugar, shake, shake, shake.

 It's for my dinner today.

 Pour a little chocolate sauce, yum, yum. Pour a little chocolate sauce, yum, yum. Pour a little chocolate sauce, yum, yum.

 It's for my dinner today.

 Eat a juicy pancake, munch, munch, munch. Eat a juicy pancake, munch, munch, munch. Eat a juicy pancake, munch, munch, munch.

 It's for my dinner today.

In the Springtime

 Spring is a symbol of new life such as an arrival of newborn chicks...

 and the baby lambs frolicking in the fields.

 Can you see the colourful spring flowers brightening up the land?

 Can you smell the sweet blossom on the fruit trees?

 Can you hear the tuneful sound of the birds?

 April will still bring many showers.

 But we can feel the warmth of the sunshine.

 Maybe you can stay still and enjoy this special time.

Grandad Grows Potatoes

 Every year, Grandad plants potatoes in his garden bed.

 The rain waters them so that they are fed.

 The sun brings warmth throughout the day,

 while Grandad watches to keep the pests at bay.

 Soon, green shoots appear in sight.

 But we must wait patiently until the time is right

 to dig up the potatoes straight from the ground.

 All shapes and sizes – large, small, oval and round.

 Wash them, cook them, pop them in a dish.

 To eat fresh from the garden with whatever you wish.

Remember, Remember the Fifth of November

 The Catherine Wheel sparkles brightly as it spins faster and faster.

 Children are using sparklers to write their names in the air.

 Rockets blast high into the sky.

 The last firework is spectacular!

 Explosions fill the sky with light and colour.

 The smoke clears.

 You can hear bangers and fire crackers all around you.

 All is calm once more.

Countdown to Christmas

 Christmas is coming; it's time to get ready.

 Let's start by getting our Christmas tree.

 Let's decorate it first with colourful baubles. We will place them carefully one-by-one.

 Now for the lights twinkling brightly.

 Then it's time to add the tinsel, laying it gently over all of the branches.

 The shiny star is placed at the top so that the Christmas tree is complete.

 But wait! What about the presents to put under the tree? Can you see the ball?

 And don't forget to hang up your stocking before you go to bed,

 because Christmas Day will soon be here!

In Your Imagination

- Can you Hear the Music?
- Ahoy There!
- Fun at the Fair
- Kelly's Balloon Ride
- Flash the Aeroplane
- The Circus Comes to Town

Can You Hear the Music?

 Sssh! Listen... Can you hear the music?

 The soft tinkling of the flutes,

 and the loud blast of the trumpets.

 The sudden clash of the cymbals.

 Let's lean closer... What else we can hear?

 The music stops.

 And suddenly everyone starts to clap!

 George is blind so cannot see the musicians,

 but he knows all the sounds of the different instruments as the orchestra starts to play again.

 'Close your eyes,' he whispers to his friends, 'and start to dream...'

Ahoy There!

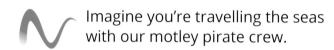 Imagine you're travelling the seas with our motley pirate crew.

 The Captain walks proudly on deck and surveys the ocean ahead.

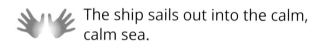 The ship sails out into the calm, calm sea.

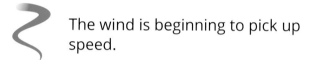 The wind is beginning to pick up speed.

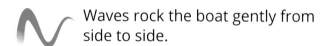 Waves rock the boat gently from side to side.

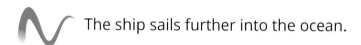 The ship sails further into the ocean.

Seagulls fly high above you.

 'Hoist the mainsail!' shout the men.

Spray starts to fall onto the wooden deck of the boat.

 Use all of your strength and swim to the ship.

 The Jolly Roger flies proudly at the top of the mast.

 You all climb safely aboard the trusty ship.

 Treasure Island lies ahead!

 The treasure is safely stowed away below deck.

 Quick, run! Look for the treasure! Here it is...

 The pirates roll up their map, ready for their next adventure.

Fun at the Fair

 It's a lovely sunny day.

 and start to skip on down.

 The Fair has come to town.

 Where will you start?

 You hold your friend's hand tight

 The horses on the carousel are moving up and down.

Listen to the squeals of joy on the Dodgems

 and the shrieks of fear as the ghost train appears.

 Time for candyfloss as the lights start to shine.

 Playing 'throw the hoop' before going home.

 Will you win a prize? What would you like?

 Something to take home and cuddle tonight!

Kelly's Balloon Ride

 Kelly dreams of an adventure in a hot air balloon.

 across the fields and rivers,

 She imagines the roar of the gas,

 away from the trees,

 as it fills up the balloon.

 and around the lakes.

 Slowly, slowly, up it goes,

 High above the winding paths,

and jumping animals,

 the people all seem like tiny toys, as they go about their day.

 The train looks like a snake curling its way across the land

 and the birds become her friends,

 as they fly alongside,

 and keep her company until it is time to go home.

Flash the Aeroplane

 Flash the Aeroplane sits on the runway.

 The pilot is on board checking all of the controls.

 Flash wonders where in the world they will go today?

 The passengers climb on board.

 The engines rev up loudly!

 Flash picks up speed...

 up, up, up in the sky they go,

 above the white fluffy clouds,

 above the earth.

 This is where Flash is happiest of all.

The Circus Comes to Town

 Roll up... Roll up...

 The Circus is here!

 Jugglers catch balls flying through the air.

 Clowns make everyone laugh at their tricks.

 Strongmen lift heavy weights.

 Then the audience is very quiet...

 The trapeze artists climb higher and higher,

 and swing upside down, and from side to side.

 Everyone stands to clap and cheer.

 Hurrah for the Circus!

Adding a Personal Touch

- Let's Bake a Birthday Cake
- Freddie's Bathtime
- Ben Goes on the Bus
- Olly Goes Fishing
- Alice Plays Football
- Team Effort

Let's Bake a Birthday Cake

 We take a big round bowl.

 In goes the soft, slippery butter.

 Next, we sprinkle in the sugar.

 Then we crack one egg, two eggs, three eggs.

 Now, we add flour, which looks like soft, falling snow.

 We fold the mixture together.

 Into the warm oven goes Kate's birthday cake,

 until the timer goes ping!

 Just in time for tea.

Happy Birthday, Kate!

Freddie's Bathtime

 Splish, splash, splosh.
Splish, splash, splosh.

 Freddie's having fun!

 Freddie's in the bath!

 Squeeze the sponge.
Squeeze the sponge.

 Catching bubbles.
Catching bubbles.

 Freddie's getting clean!

Rub with the towel.
Rub with the towel.

 Freddie's feeling sleepy.

 Freddie's warm and dry.

 Climb into bed.
Climb into bed.

 Brush your teeth.
Brush your teeth.

 Freddie's fast asleep.

Ben Goes on the Bus

 Ben and Mummy walk to the bus stop.

 Ben sees his friend Max and waves.

 When the bus arrives, they climb up the stairs to the top.

 The bus goes up the hill. It is very slow.

 They sit right at the front.

 Then they go down the hill. Wheeeeeee!

 Ben can feel the big wheels turning as the bus begins to move.

 Ben loves going on the bus!

Olly Goes Fishing

 It's a bright sunny day.

 And before we know it, we catch 1, 2, 3 fish.

 Over bumpy tracks we drive.

 We look back at the beautiful lake.

 We squelch along the path.

 We squelch back along the path.

 Then there is a beautiful lake.

 Over bumpy tracks we drive.

 We cast our line.

 What a happy day!

Alice Plays Football

 Ellie and her friends are playing football in the park.

 Then, Lottie calls for Alice to join the game.

 Alice sits down quietly to watch. She feels too shy to join in.

 Alice's heart begins to beat quickly.

 She looks on as they dodge and swerve,

 Alice runs on to the pitch.

 kick and run and jump.

 Ellie passes the ball to Alice who kicks it high into the air.

Lauren runs towards the goal

 Backwards and forwards it goes, up and down the pitch.

 and POW! It's a header, straight in.

 Alice kicks and runs and jumps.

 Then, the ball is kicked back into the game.

 Alice is having fun!

Team Effort

 The Downshill Dodgers basketball team are feeling excited.

 The crowd cheers and shouts; they jump up and down,

 It is the day of the big game against their rivals.

 as all the players try their hardest.

 They put on their jerseys and wish each other good luck.

 Time goes quickly and the game is nearly over.

 The whistle blows and play begins.

 Jack bounces the ball.

Then he passes it to Will.

 Will shoots...

 Will catches the ball and holds it tight.

 and scores!

 He moves his wheelchair towards the basket. Faster and faster he goes.

 Downshill Dodgers have won the game!

Hands-on Learning

- Walking on the Moon
- Great Fire of London
- Deep in the Rainforest
- Greek Myths
- Winding Rivers
- Growing Sunflowers

Walking on the Moon

 The moon rotates around the earth in a circle called an orbit.

 The moon has no weather so there is no wind

 People have looked up to the sky and wondered about the moon for thousands of years.

 and there is no rain.

 Then, in July 1969, two astronauts walked on the surface of the moon for the very first time.

 This means the footprints of Neil Armstrong and Buzz Aldrin

 The moon has no atmosphere so the astronauts weighed much less than on earth. They could jump up very high in the air.

 will remain for millions of years to come.

Great Fire of London

 In 1666, a baker in Pudding Lane

 The streets were narrow and there was no fire brigade.

 accidentally started a fire.

 People and rats ran away!

 It lasted 1, 2, 3, 4, 5 days.

 Buildings collapsed to the ground.

 The fire spread quickly across the city.

 Eventually the fire burned itself out and the city was still again.

Deep in the Rainforest

 Rainforests grow along the equator in the areas called the Tropics.

 They are hot and wet all year round.

 It rains almost every day in the rainforest.

 Some animals like the rain.

 Others try very hard to avoid getting wet.

 Rainforests grow in layers.

 At the very top is the emergent layer, where the tallest trees poke out.

 Beneath is a thick layer of trees called the canopy.

Below is the understorey, made up of smaller trees and saplings.

 The giant anaconda can grow to a massive eight metres in length.

 The rainforest is home to at least half of the world's species of animals and plants.

 It is more than a metre around its middle and weighs a quarter of a tonne.

 The jaguar likes to creep up on its prey.

 The squirrel monkeys enjoy climbing the trees and leaping from branch to branch.

 Some snakes slither their bodies from side to side. They like to live in trees as well as in the water.

 Rainforest frogs like to jump from place to place too.

The parrots and butterflies have such colourful wings.

 The laziest animal in the rainforest is the sloth.

 It will spend 18 hours a day hanging upside down fast asleep!

 The mountain gorillas from the Central African rainforest

 are endangered because of forest clearance and poaching for their meat.

 There are now fewer than 40,000 left.

 The rainforest, its people, animals and plants are at risk from human destruction.

 If we really care about our rainforests then we must try to protect them!

Greek Myths

 Feel the brushing wings of Pegasus.

 Avoid the slithering hair of Medusa.

 Feel his gentle steps.

 Watch out! You'll be turned to stone.

 Evade the nips of the Cerberus

 Be sure to look at your reflection in the shield.

 as you tiptoe past the gates.

 Look for Perseus' footprints.

Welcome Perseus, washed ashore.

 Look around the Labyrinth.

 Hear the wings of the Harpy.

 Unwind the ball of string and find your way out.

 See her long, long hair.

 Watch out for the Minotaur's horns!

Winding Rivers

 The source of a river is high up in the mountains.

The river falls steeply over a short distance, forming waterfalls.

The river usually flows quickly, down steep slopes.

It continues its descent through a narrow v-shaped valley.

The river follows a zig-zag course, producing interlocking spurs as it erodes the landscape.

 The river now receives more water from tributaries, which join it.

As the river gets larger, it transports large loads of material with it.

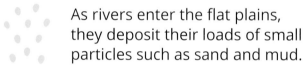 As rivers enter the flat plains, they deposit their loads of small particles such as sand and mud.

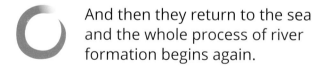 And then they return to the sea and the whole process of river formation begins again.

Growing Sunflowers

 Today we prepare the soil.

 Then we sprinkle in the seeds.

 We water the seeds.

 Now we watch the sunflowers grow very slowly. They grow taller and taller towards the sky.

 See how the sunflowers follow the sun.

 What bright and happy flowers.

 Let's stop for a moment.

 And enjoy the beautiful colours.

Time for Talking

- Animal Friends
- A Safe Place
- The Inquisitive Iguanodon
- The Frightened Ghost
- First Day at Forest School

Animal Friends

 Sammy Sea Bird flies around the world to meet his friends.

 In America, Bear pads through the forest to greet him.

 In England, Rabbit hops across a field to say 'hello'.

 In China, Panda dozes peacefully.

 In Australia, Koala climbs a tree, and waves at him.

 In Africa, Giraffe is eating delicious leaves

 and Lion roars very loudly.

 In India, Elephant is playful and sprinkles water everywhere.

 Sammy smiles and laughs, then flies home.

 All Sammy's friends are different and that's what makes them special!

A Safe Place

 A little red squirrel lived in the woodland on an island,

 Sometimes she would hop from branch to bough,

 surrounded by the sea.

 looking for pinecones to eat.

 A little red squirrel lived in a drey, a nest made of sticks and leaves,

 At other times she would scurry about the roots,

 high up in a tree.

 searching for places to store nuts and seeds.

But she knew that whenever the rain started to pour,

 and skies turned to grey...

 she could run up the tree,

 and climb into her drey.

 Here she feels safe and calm,

 far away from harm.

The Inquisitive Iguanodon

 Once upon a time, over a hundred million years ago,

 and clawed at the sticks,

 Iggy and his brother and sister were out playing,

 and poked at the egg.

 when they came across an enormous egg laying in a bed of leaves and sticks.

 They wanted to find out what was inside.

 They nibbled on the leaves,

 Iggy walked round and round.

He patted it with his nose.

 in between the bushes and trees,

 He flicked it with his tail again, and again,

 until it landed with a soft thud at the bottom.

 and pushed the egg out of the nest.

 The egg cracked and out popped their new baby sister – so that was what was inside the egg!

 Down the hill it rolled,

The Frightened Ghost

 Jessie and Jacob are scared of ghosts.

 Will they be creeping up the stairs?

 They look for them everywhere!

 Where can they hide?

 Are they hiding under the bed?

 They look, they listen...nothing there.

 Will they be floating up high?

 Maybe the ghosts are frightened of them?

 Dancing on the ceiling?

First Day at Forest School

 The animals are getting ready for their first day at Forest School.

 Hedgehog is nervous and curls up into a little ball.

 Deer is feeling shy; will he look different with his very long legs?

 When the others see Hedgehog, they say 'WOW, that's a great trick!'

 Squirrel is excited about playtime, especially showing his favourite game, hide and seek, to his friends.

 And Hedgehog stops feeling nervous; he feels calm and ready.

 Badger is tired and grumpy because he didn't sleep well last night.

 They all walk to school together thinking 'This is going to be a good day!'

About the Authors

Mary Atkinson and Sandra Hooper have collaborated since 2007 to help promote positive touch activities for all children.

Photo Credit: Sarah Ketelaars

Mary is an award-winning complementary therapist and author of four books on massage including *Healing Touch for Children* (Gaia 2009). Sandra is an experienced primary school teacher, massage therapist and a respected international trainer on the Massage in Schools Programme (MISP).

Mary and Sandra run training courses for individuals and organisations to help develop the skills and confidence to use their ten massage strokes to create story massages appropriate to varying situations and circumstances. These sessions, which are suitable for anyone who has an interest in encouraging positive touch for children, can be tailored to suit your particular needs. The training is also excellent continuing education for already trained MISP instructors who wish to have more ideas for working with story massage.

For more information on the authors, the training opportunities and inspiring updates on story massage projects around the world please look at the website and blog:

www.storymassage.co.uk

Endorsements

'Story Massage empowers parents giving them a tool they can use to interact with their children in a calm non-threatening way. It is also a way for parents to spend one to one time with their child thus reinforcing the bond between parent and child.'

– Andrea Bilbow, OBE, Chief Executive, ADDISS, The National Attention Deficit Disorder Information and Support Service, UK

'This beautiful technique is an easy to grasp concept that can be passed and shared with others very simply. It is going to be something that we can use all the time.'

– Louise Anderson, Mum and Social Worker

'I find the whole concept simple but extremely effective. The ability to have ten strokes to cover so many objects, feelings and actions allows me to see how it can be used in a variety of settings.'

– Carla Malkett, Rachel House Children's Hospice, UK

'I would recommend this book to anyone who would like to help children learn to relax at home, school, nursery, play group, in groups or one to one. It introduces simple massage skills to promote relaxation and well-being. The stories help promote creativity, turn taking, empathy and self-esteem. Great concept, great book.'

– *Kay Locke, Yoga Therapist for Mental Health and Special Needs*

'I work in a special needs early years setting with children who have profound and multiple learning disabilities and also some with sensory processing disorders and some with challenging behaviour.

We have trialled a few of these massage rhymes and stories. Some children showed real enjoyment and relaxed into the sessions, others stilled and briefly calmed down, others nuzzled into staff showing pleasure as they had their massage and some lifted up their tops by themselves during it to get skin on skin contact. For other children it was another alternative idea for them to get used to "touch" and they tolerated and preferred some strokes more than others, again, that is positive in itself. As it has been so successful we are now going to extend it into our timetable on a regular basis.'

– *Helen Edgar, Special Needs Teacher, UK*

'The book is AMAZING! I love it! It's so easy to use as a teacher.'

– Mary Spink, Drama Teacher, Massage in Schools Programme Instructor

'The reach of positive touch never ceases to amaze me. All it takes are some bold and visionary advocates, in this case from the folks at Story Massage UK. This totally innovative program empowers children using structured touch for interpersonal skills development, confidence building and self-discovery.'

– David Palmer, Founder and Executive Director of TouchPro International, US

'We have been using story massage with our pupils for twelve months. The pupils at Westfield have a wide range of complex needs and we have found that there are benefits for all pupils from 4 years to 19 years. The main benefits for us have been increased levels of engagement, understanding and acceptance of appropriate touch, peer working across phases and the enhancement of our literacy curriculum. Story massage is very effective and very easy to put in place across a school.'

– Nicki Gilbert, Head Teacher, Westfield Special School, UK